BUILD BACK BETTER SECTOR GUIDES
VOLUME 1: OVERVIEW

OCTOBER 2024

ASIAN DEVELOPMENT BANK

 Creative Commons Attribution 3.0 IGO license (CC BY 3.0 IGO)

© 2024 Asian Development Bank
6 ADB Avenue, Mandaluyong City, 1550 Metro Manila, Philippines
Tel +63 2 8632 4444; Fax +63 2 8636 2444
www.adb.org

Some rights reserved. Published in 2024.

ISBN 978-92-9270-937-2 (print); 978-92-9270-938-9 (PDF); 978-92-9270-939-6 (ebook)
Publication Stock No. TIM240435-2
DOI: http://dx.doi.org/10.22617/TIM240435-2

The views expressed in this publication are those of the authors and do not necessarily reflect the views and policies of the Asian Development Bank (ADB) or its Board of Governors or the governments they represent.

ADB does not guarantee the accuracy of the data included in this publication and accepts no responsibility for any consequence of their use. The mention of specific companies or products of manufacturers does not imply that they are endorsed or recommended by ADB in preference to others of a similar nature that are not mentioned.

By making any designation of or reference to a particular territory or geographic area in this document, ADB does not intend to make any judgments as to the legal or other status of any territory or area.

This publication is available under the Creative Commons Attribution 3.0 IGO license (CC BY 3.0 IGO) https://creativecommons.org/licenses/by/3.0/igo/. By using the content of this publication, you agree to be bound by the terms of this license. For attribution, translations, adaptations, and permissions, please read the provisions and terms of use at https://www.adb.org/terms-use#openaccess.

This CC license does not apply to non-ADB copyright materials in this publication. If the material is attributed to another source, please contact the copyright owner or publisher of that source for permission to reproduce it. ADB cannot be held liable for any claims that arise as a result of your use of the material.

Please contact pubsmarketing@adb.org if you have questions or comments with respect to content, or if you wish to obtain copyright permission for your intended use that does not fall within these terms, or for permission to use the ADB logo.

Corrigenda to ADB publications may be found at http://www.adb.org/publications/corrigenda.

Notes:
In this publication, "$" refers to United States dollars.
All photos by ADB.

Cover design by Jan Carlo Dela Cruz.

CONTENTS

TABLES AND BOXES

FOREWORD

Asia and the Pacific bears the largest share of the world's disaster impacts, with 36% of worldwide natural hazard events occurring in Asian Development Bank (ADB) developing member countries (DMCs) from 2004 to 2023. The brunt of disaster impacts falls disproportionately upon poor and vulnerable populations and can generate long-term setbacks to sustainable economic development.

Failure of infrastructure due to insufficient resilience contributes significantly to disaster-related losses and hampers recovery efforts. The trend of increasing disaster losses across the region underscores the continued importance of investing in resilience as a central tenet of recovery and reconstruction. Rather than reconfiguring vulnerability, transforming countries toward resilient long-term development pathways by building back better is critical to prepare for tomorrow's challenges.

Over the last two decades, ADB's support for post-disaster recovery and reconstruction has comprised a relatively small, yet highly impactful share of our portfolio. In 2019, a review of ADB's 2004 Disaster and Emergency Assistance Policy identified a wealth of insights and lessons learned on "build back better," a core principle for all ADB's post-disaster assistance. Alongside growing disaster impacts and climate change trends, the relevance of building back better has increased even more in recent years.

In 2021, ADB approved a revised Disaster and Emergency Assistance Policy, which seeks to enhance the efficiency and impact of ADB's support to DMCs to strengthen resilience to disasters and emergencies, with build back better retained as a core principle. In October 2024 ADB published its *Disaster Risk Management Action Plan, 2024–2030: Redoubling Action towards Disaster Resilience,* which sets out ADB's approach and workstreams for achieving disaster resilience in Asia and the Pacific. The policy review process inspired a highly collaborative, OneADB effort to capture internal and external best practices on climate and disaster-resilient recovery in the form of these practical, solutions-oriented *Build Back Better Sector Guides.* I greatly appreciate the ADB country teams, sector offices, and DMC counterparts that contributed their knowledge and experience to these guides in a truly collaborative approach.

As Asia and the Pacific's climate bank, ADB is committed to redoubling efforts on disaster risk management and scaling up climate adaptation investments in order to build a prosperous, inclusive, resilient, and sustainable future for our DMCs. With these guides, ADB hopes to make a practical contribution to the global knowledge base and enable those working in a post-disaster context to place resilience at the center of recovery.

Bruno Carrasco
Director General, Climate Change and Sustainable Development Department
Asian Development Bank

ACKNOWLEDGMENTS

Preparation of this *Build Back Better Sector Guides* series was led by Belinda Hewitt, senior disaster risk management specialist, Climate Change and Sustainable Development Department (CCSD), ADB with substantive inputs and review from Brigitte Balthasar, senior disaster and climate risk financing specialist, CCSD, ADB; Charlotte Benson, former principal disaster risk management Specialist, ADB; Alexandra Galperin, unit head, disaster risk management, CCSD, ADB; Steven Goldfinch, senior disaster risk management specialist, CCSD, ADB; Anne Orquiza, senior disaster risk management officer, CCSD, ADB; Grendel Saldevar, senior operations assistant, CCSD, ADB; and Mario Unterwaining, former disaster risk management specialist (resilient infrastructure), ADB. The series was developed in close collaboration with ADB Sectors Group and country teams. Margie Peters-Fawcett copy edited the volumes with the assistance of Cherry Lynn Zafaralla as proofreader. Layout was created by Rommel Marilla, page proofs checking by Levi Rodolfo Lusterio, and administrative support by Michelle Imperial.

Paul Venton led the drafting of the content for this volume with written inputs from Charlotte Benson; Alessio Giardino, senior climate change specialist, CCSD, ADB; Steven Goldfinch; Amir Jilani, social sector specialist, Sectors Group (SG), ADB; Belinda Hewitt; Joel V. Mangahas, principal country specialist, Southeast Asia Regional Department, ADB; Madhavi Pundit, senior economist, Economic Research and Development Impact Department, ADB; Karin Schelzig, director, SG, ADB, Herman van der Most; Ashwin Hosur Viswanath, senior project officer (urban), SG; and Geoffrey Wilson, senior water resources specialist, SG. Peer review by Amir Gilani and Tsutomu Nifuku of Miyamoto International is greatly appreciated. The ADB Department of Communications and Knowledge Management supervised the publication of the series.

ABBREVIATIONS

ADB	Asian Development Bank
BBB	build back better
DMC	developing member country
DRM	disaster risk management
DRR	disaster risk reduction
EAL	Emergency Assistance Loan
EWS	early warning system
IFRM	integrated flood risk management
O&M	operation and maintenance
PDNA	post-disaster needs assessment

A family crosses the flooded streets of Pakistan during the floods of 2010.

I

INTRODUCTION

Timely support for recovery and reconstruction efforts is critical when a disaster occurs to minimize any potential long-term setbacks to sustainable and inclusive socioeconomic development. It is essential to provide a window of opportunity to rebuild assets and improve livelihoods to increase climate and disaster resilience and reduce the risk of future hazards. With impacts of disasters projected to rise in the coming decades as affected by climate change, unplanned urbanization, poor risk governance, and a range of other trends, challenges relating to climate uncertainty, growing complexity of infrastructure systems, and the compounding nature of multiple hazard events underline the importance of ensuring that communities and infrastructure systems are equipped to cope, adapt, and recover when faced with future shocks and stresses.

Developing member countries (DMCs) of the Asian Development Bank (ADB) bear a disproportionate share of impacts from geophysical and extreme weather hazard events. Between 2004 and 2023, these DMCs accounted for 55% of global disaster fatalities and 74% of people affected.[1] Over this 20-year period, ADB has provided more than $9.1 billion in financing for emergency assistance loan (EAL) projects relating to disasters triggered by natural hazards, conflict, displacement, food insecurity, and health emergencies. The support that ADB offers its DMCs aims at ensuring resilient post-disaster recovery, as well as strengthening long-term disaster risk reduction (DRR).

ADB's Strategy 2030[2] and 2021 Disaster and Emergency Assistance Policy[3] outline commitments to ensure effective response and support to build back better (BBB) after a disaster or emergency.[4] Build back better refers to the use of the early recovery and reconstruction phases after a disaster or emergency to increase resilience of nations and communities to future events by integrating risk reduction

---

1   Centre for Research on the Epidemiology of Disasters, EM-DAT: The International Disaster Database. www.emdat.be (accessed 5 February 2024). People affected by multiple disasters have been counted multiple times.
2   ADB. 2017. *Strategy 2030: Achieving a Prosperous, Inclusive, Resilient, and Sustainable Asia and the Pacific*.
3   ADB. 2021. *Revised Disaster and Emergency Assistance Policy*.
4   Strategy 2030 sets out a commitment to "provide assistance for disaster response, including support to build back better."

measures into the restoration of physical infrastructure, societal systems, livelihoods, economies, and the environment.[5] By systematically promoting risk-informed, well-designed, and timely recovery and reconstruction, ADB supports the implementation of international agreements, such as the Sendai Framework for Disaster Risk Reduction, 2015–2030 and the 2030 Agenda for Sustainable Development Goals, including its 17 Sustainable Development Goals, both of which promote a comprehensive approach toward disaster risk management (DRM) and BBB frameworks, including through community-based applications.

The six volumes that comprise the *Build Back Better Sector Guides* series aim to support ADB staff, consultants, and DMC counterparts to enhance the climate and disaster resilience of DMC communities, infrastructure, and systems through effective and well-designed post-disaster assistance. The volumes are based on principles, measures, and lessons learned from the international BBB literature; a review of over 40 ADB EALs processed between 2004 and 2021; and the outcome of consultations with a wide range of ADB staff.

Each of the volumes has been co-developed with relevant ADB sector and thematic groups. The sectors are areas in which ADB has played a key role in post-disaster recovery and reconstruction and where majority of ADB's disaster and emergency assistance has focused in the last 20 years. They are as follows:

(i)   Volume 1: Overview
(ii)   Volume 2: Transport
(iii) Volume 3: Water, Sanitation, and Hygiene (WASH)
(iv)   Volume 4: Irrigated Agriculture
(v)   Volume 5: Social Infrastructure
(vi)   Volume 6: Power

This Volume 1: Overview covers the broad measures that are likely relevant to any post-disaster recovery and reconstruction project, regardless of sector.

The scope of this series includes building resilience in response to disasters triggered by natural hazards; however, some of its content is relevant to the broader aspect of economic recovery, including within the context of health emergencies and conflict. Complementary objectives, including equity and inclusion, green recovery, poverty reduction, and broader sustainable development, are also presented.

---

[5]   Adapted from United Nations General Assembly. 2016. Report of the Open-Ended Intergovernmental Expert Working Group on Indicators and Terminology Relating to DRR. Seventy-First Session, Item 19(c).

ADB's Role in Resilient Post-Disaster Recovery and Reconstruction

Following a disaster, ADB can mobilize rapid post-disaster technical support under the second window of its Asia Pacific Disaster Response Fund in areas such as the preparation of post-disaster needs assessments; government-led recovery plans; and post-disaster projects, EALs included. The PDNA is a well-established tailored methodology that is used for analyzing damage, loss, and needs prioritization. While the exercise should be led by the government, it is often conducted with the support of one or more international partners. The PDNA compiles information relating to the physical impacts of a disaster, economic value of damages and losses, human and macroeconomic impacts, and cost of early and long-term recovery needs and priorities. As such, the PDNA is an important tool to inform implementation of BBB through post-disaster programming.

Once recovery and reconstruction requirements have been assessed, ADB can mobilize finance for recovery and reconstruction through EAL, additional financing for pre-established projects, and investment projects that support longer-term reconstruction needs. ADB's 2021 Emergency Assistance Loan Policy enables the rapid approval of loans (within 12 weeks) to assist in the rebuilding of high-priority physical assets and the restoration of economic, social, and governance activities following disasters triggered by natural hazards, health emergencies, food insecurity, technological and industrial accidents, and post-conflict situations.[6] The Emergency Assistance Loan Policy and the 2021 Disaster and Emergency Assistance Policy aim to support DMC's BBB efforts to enhance climate and disaster resilience. Table 1 provides a list of additional resources relating to ADB's policies and directives relating to post-disaster assistance.

Table 1: Key Documents on ADB Policies and Guidance for Post-Disaster Assistance

Document	Web Page
2021 Disaster and Emergency Assistance Policy	https://www.adb.org/documents/revised-disaster-and-emergency-assistance-policy
Revised Emergency Assistance Loan Policy	https://www.adb.org/documents/revised-emergency-assistance-loan-policy
Establishment of a Second Window of Assistance under the Asia Pacific Disaster Response Fund	https://www.adb.org/documents/establishment-second-window-assistance-under-asia-pacific-disaster-response-fund
Post-Disaster Needs Assessment Guidelines	https://recovery.preventionweb.net/build-back-better/post-disaster-needs-assessments
Disaster Recovery Planning: Explanatory Note and Case Study	https://www.adb.org/sites/default/files/publication/885861/disaster-recovery-planning-explanatory-note-case-study.pdf

Source: Asian Development Bank.

---

[6]   ADB. 2021. *Revised Emergency Assistance Loan Policy*.

Importance of Long-Term Resilience Building

Long-term and upstream approaches to resilience building are critical to minimize the impacts of disasters and ensure more effective and efficient use of post-disaster assistance resources. ADB can play a key role in leveraging increased risk awareness to ensure resilience-focused upstream planning. Where risk-responsive socioeconomic development and sector plans are already in place ahead of a disaster, they can more effectively guide long-term disaster recovery and bring about a shift toward resilience and sustainable development.

Risk-informed sector plans enable more rapid and effective post-disaster recovery and reconstruction where they are informed by comprehensive multihazard disaster risk assessments and incorporate ex ante recovery planning. Past ADB EALs, such as the 2015 Nepal: Earthquake Emergency Assistance Project (see Volume 5: Social Infrastructure) and the 2018 Tonga: Cyclone Gita Recovery Project (see Volume 6: Power), aligned recovery planning with climate and disaster resilience objectives set out in existing sector programs, government road maps, and the national development plan.

Disaster risk financing solutions address fiscal impacts and economic losses triggered by natural hazards and support countries to increase their financial resilience. Hence, they are another key mechanism to enable long-term resilience building. When addressing all risk layers, disaster risk financing solutions can contribute to the financing of post-disaster recovery and reconstruction actions as well; however, disaster risk financing is not within the scope of this series, as it focuses on effective and well-designed post-disaster recovery and reconstruction.

Use of the Build Back Better Sector Guides

This introductory volume comprises the principles and crosscutting measures that are likely relevant to any post-disaster recovery and reconstruction project, regardless of sector. All users of the series are encouraged to review this volume first.

The volume provides an overview of good practice solutions, considerations, and lessons learned for building back better, but does not represent a step-by-step handbook on methods to prepare and implement post-disaster needs assessments or EALs; nor does it for other forms of post-disaster assistance. For any given project, it is important that resilience measures are selected appropriately and on a project-by-project basis, informed by an understanding of the project activities and local context. There should be analysis of current and future risk; economic development objectives; economic feasibility and viability; as well as relevant policies, including climate and disaster risk management and safeguards requirements. Each volume provides references for various additional technical resources that can support project-specific decision-making.

Children cooking in shelters made with indigenous materials, in the aftermath of the 2015 earthquake in Nepal.

ADB Philippines: KALAHI-CIDSS National Community-Driven Development Project (46420-002), Social Protection Support Project (Additional Financing) (43407-014), and Countercyclical Support Loan (43300-013). Scenes from Barangay Katipunan, Pilar, Surigao Del Norte. Many families from the barangay are recipients of the Conditional Cash Transfer (4Ps) program. Several small infrastructure in the barangay were also funded by the Kalahi-CIDSS program.

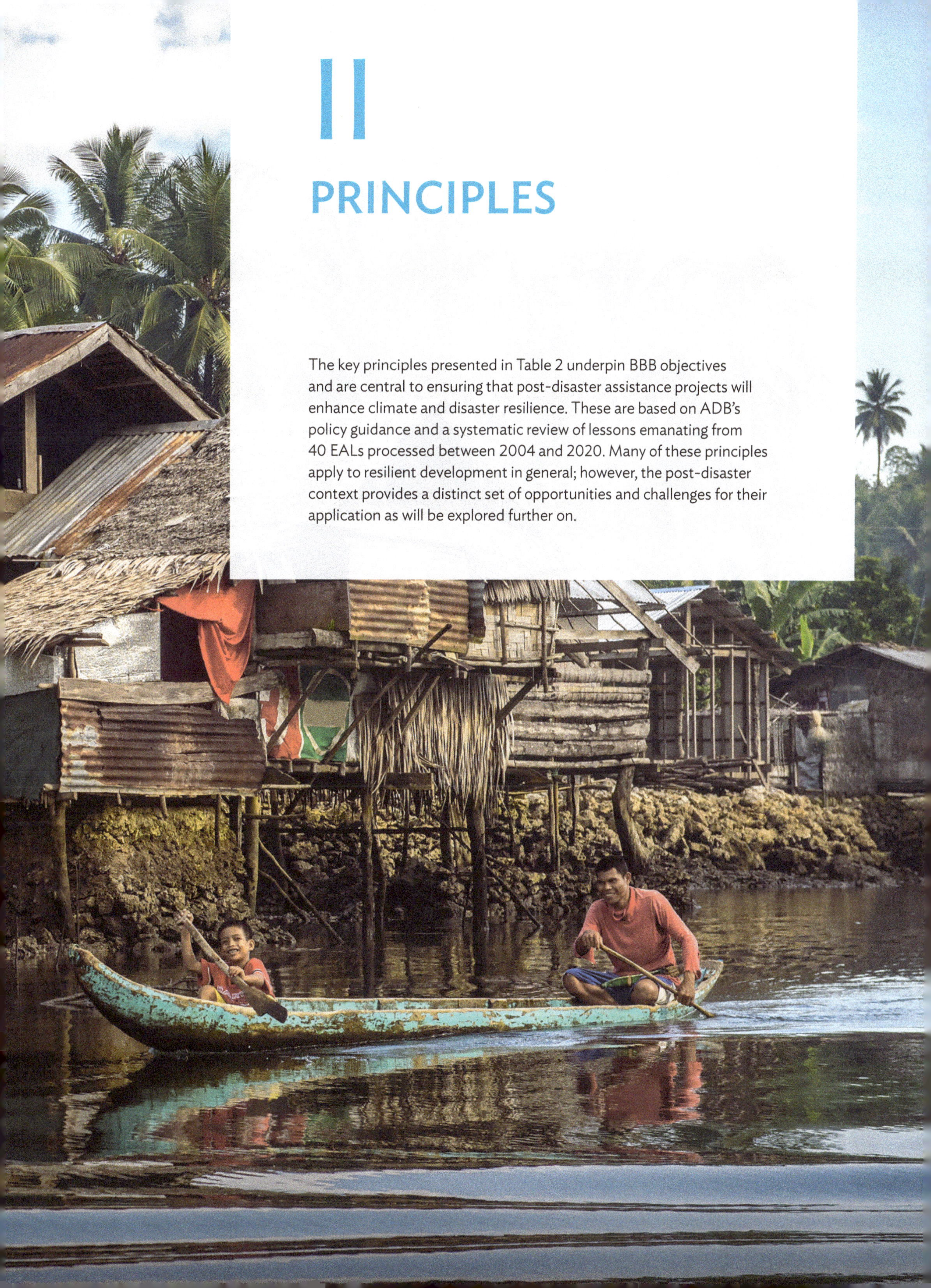

II

PRINCIPLES

The key principles presented in Table 2 underpin BBB objectives and are central to ensuring that post-disaster assistance projects will enhance climate and disaster resilience. These are based on ADB's policy guidance and a systematic review of lessons emanating from 40 EALs processed between 2004 and 2020. Many of these principles apply to resilient development in general; however, the post-disaster context provides a distinct set of opportunities and challenges for their application as will be explored further on.

Table 2: Key Principles in Build Back Better

Risk reduction	**Minimize exposure and vulnerability to natural hazards according to an up-to-date understanding of climate and disaster risk.** Effective recovery must leave communities safer than they previously were whereby their exposure and vulnerability has been reduced. At times, this leads to difficult decisions on whether or not to rebuild and, if so, where. It is essential that meaningful consultations be held with a wide range of local stakeholders, and that the socioeconomic implications for communities and user groups are well thought out. Given that climate change, population growth, and urbanization are dynamic and can evolve rapidly, it is critical to ensure that risk reduction solutions allow the capacity or flexibility to accommodate future risk and address uncertainties, particularly for reconstruction and recovery efforts that result in changes to physical or social systems that are locked in for the long term. Post-disaster data collection and monitoring of reconstruction activities can also provide valuable information for risk reduction and implementation of build back better (BBB).
Capacity development and knowledge	**Enhance the capacity of individuals, communities, and institutions to cope and adapt when disaster occurs.** By definition, a disaster or emergency indicates that local capacity is overwhelmed. Therefore, it is important to strengthen the capacity of individuals, communities, and institutions so that they can recover more rapidly, effectively, and efficiently in the future, and to ensure that resilience solutions can be sustainably operated, maintained, and scaled up in the long term. Capacity development should be considered as a stand-alone project output and include, for instance, training and institutional strengthening using a participative approach. Communities, government planners, and private sector actors all need awareness and understanding of the hazards they face to make decisions that will reduce their exposure and vulnerability. Capacity building can also serve to enhance the available pool of individuals that can respond to future disasters.
Local leadership	**Support communities and local stakeholders to drive their own recovery.** Many disaster recovery processes tend to be centrally planned and implemented in a top-down manner. In cases where communities are not adequately involved, there is greater risk that recovery and reconstruction efforts will be inappropriate or unsustainable. Stakeholder consultation alone is not likely to adequately address the issues. Therefore, communities and other key stakeholders should be involved in the decision-making process and project implementation so as to establish buy-in and ownership; capture valuable local knowledge (e.g., local disaster risks); and build long-term capacity to plan and deliver positive outcomes. Such practice will not only generate significant long-term social resilience but also enhance the sustainability and impact of recovery programming. Community-driven development is one such example.
Inclusion and equity	**Ensure that building resilience will benefit those most vulnerable to disasters.** Women, those with disabilities, poor people, older adults, and other vulnerable and marginalized groups bear a disproportionate share of disaster impacts, both due to inherent vulnerabilities and because they tend to occupy settings with high disaster exposure and vulnerability. Post-disaster assistance must be built on the principle of "leave no one behind." When seeking to build climate and disaster resilience, inclusion bears the question "resilience for whom?" to ensure that vulnerable groups are placed at the center of the recovery process. They can do so by being encouraged to participate and thus empowered as agents of change.

continued on next page

Table 2 *continued*

Quality	**Provide rigorous quality control of climate and disaster resilience measures to prevent further disaster risk.** Reconstruction to higher levels of resilience may require introduction of new materials (e.g., concrete road pavement) or design standards (e.g., normative provisions for natural hazards) for which there may be an absence of local knowledge and skills. Project implementation in itself is highly challenging in the post-disaster context; projects may be faced with a significant shortage of raw materials and labor, as well as suffer from complex stakeholder coordination and extreme time pressures. It is essential to ensure that project designs incorporate adequate international support, capacity building, construction oversight, and commissioning to ensure that resilience measures are adequately implemented with due quality and are sustainable; and to avoid generating new physical and reputational risks in the case of future infrastructure failure.
Innovation and technology	**Promote change that brings value.** Recovery and reconstruction provide opportunities to adopt new technologies and solutions for effective recovery and long-term climate and disaster resilience. Innovation is supported by close collaboration, cross-regional knowledge sharing, and a willingness to understand the reasons for failure. At the local level, entrepreneurship is essential and is key for social and economic recovery. Innovations should be captured and shared as broadly as possible through project monitoring, reporting, and knowledge sharing.
Scalability	**Where appropriate and necessary, consider resilience solutions that can be readily scaled up for broad recovery and reconstruction.** Where there are significant and geographically dispersed reconstruction or recovery needs, it may be worth designing project components (e.g., buildings or social protection initiatives) in a manner that readily can be replicated and scaled up by government, ADB, and other development partners. Where assets are involved, they should be designed with high tolerance for human error in mind. A flexible, user-centric, and inclusive approach should be adopted in blueprints to accommodate the various local and cultural needs.

Source: Asian Development Bank.

ADB Pakistan: National Flood Emergency Response (44356-022). Nadia Qureshi, 7 years old, smiles for the camera at the volunteer run school in Pakistan Navy Relief Camp, near the town of Thatta.

III

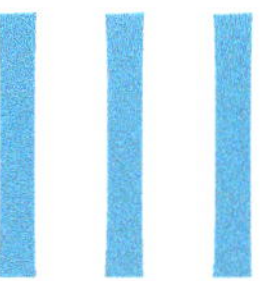

CROSSCUTTING CLIMATE AND DISASTER RESILIENCE MEASURES

Following a major disaster, restoration and reconstruction of the built environment often is the focus of the recovery effort. To enable BBB, equal priority should be given to nonstructural efforts relating to matters other than physical reconstruction, such as the strengthening of governance, planning, DRM systems, and support for resilient community recovery to reduce vulnerability to future shocks and stresses. These activities—collectively referred to in this series as "crosscutting measures"—are central to achieving resilient and inclusive socioeconomic development and reducing the impact of future disaster. Resilience measures set out in this section are intended to guide all post-disaster assistance, regardless of sector and financing modality.

Institutional Resilience Building and Governance Arrangements

Following a disaster, there are opportunities to leverage the political will of government and increased public risk awareness to revise institutional and governance arrangements to promote stronger focus on DRM, as seen in the example in Box 1. A critical review of policy strengths and gaps may enable DMCs to learn lessons from the event; recognize inherent inadequacies within existing institutional, governance, and planning arrangements; and highlight risk factors that previously may have not been considered. Addressing these elements will create an enabling environment for a recovery that is resilient with more effective systems to better respond to future disasters.

Strengthening institutional arrangements can mean either (i) the expansion of the role of an existing organization or (ii) the creation of a new, often time-bound, entity to address disaster recovery issues. Statutory or organizational arrangements for DRM that were in place prior to a disaster may prove insufficient, since legislative and/or institutional arrangements and contingency planning often focus on relief and rescue activities at the exclusion of risk reduction, recovery and reconstruction. Hence, determining which approach to support will require an initial assessment of the roles, effectiveness, and capacity of existing institutional arrangements and what additional legislative and organizational adaptations are necessary to lead, coordinate, and monitor BBB efforts.

Box 1: Project Example—Strengthening Institutional Resilience and Governance Arrangements Following the 2005 Pakistan Earthquake

To cope with challenges emerging from the 2005 earthquake, the Government of Pakistan promulgated the National Disaster Management Ordinance in 2007 to launch a comprehensive national disaster risk management (DRM) system. The ordinance outlines a three-tier system (at the national, provincial, and district levels) and called for a National Disaster Management Commission to establish policies relating to DRM. The ordinance was enacted in December 2010 and is now fully operational. As a result, the National Disaster Management Authority was created to be the central body for implementing, coordinating, and monitoring DRM at the national level.

The Earthquake Reconstruction and Rehabilitation Authority (ERRA), an autonomous statutory body, was created to coordinate efforts across government vis-á-vis the affected provinces, districts, and relevant stakeholders. ERRA's approach includes (i) strategies and standards for recovery planning; (ii) development of institutional arrangements for all levels; (iii) creation of consultative mechanisms; and (iv) undertaking of preparatory exercises, surveys, and fieldwork. Through its **Earthquake-Displaced People Livelihood Restoration Program** (40563-013), the Asian Development Bank cofinanced ERRA's program for the reconstruction of houses in earthquake-affected areas, based on seismic-resistant construction standards.

Source: ADB. Pakistan: Earthquake-Displaced People Livelihood Restoration Program.

Priority areas to strengthen governance can include formulation and revision of disaster preparedness plans as well as legislation and regulations that address urgent functions, measures, and services in the early warning phase and immediate aftermath of an event. These include declaration of a state of emergency, dissemination of early warnings, evacuation, pre-positioning first responders, mobilizing supplies and services including through easing of entry and customs requirements, etc. Other governance reform areas apply to recovery and reconstruction (e.g., administrative arrangements, fast-tracking of approvals, import and quota regulations, taxes, and duties). Last but not least, BBB rests upon the integration of DRR into sector-focused regulations and laws, among efforts to regulate land use and improve applicable codes and standards (sections III-E and III-F). Such reforms typically require sustained and systematic upstream engagement while helping to demonstrate effectiveness downstream through the reconstruction itself.

To sustain momentum, enabling adequate leadership and decision-making powers are essential, since disasters cut across political, regional, and bureaucratic lines of accountability. As discussed above, these can be achieved by strengthening existing development and sector agencies and/or creating a new agency with special powers to direct and control recovery activities. Choices should be informed by a good understanding of the political economy and hence the effectiveness of alternative arrangements for resilient recovery and risk-responsive development. Since regular planning, budgeting, procuring, and oversight practices often are temporarily suspended under national emergency legislation, there should be special arrangements in place to safeguard against corruption and mismanagement, for example by appointing a senior political or public figure who is able to take charge.[7]

---

[7]   ADB. 2018. *Institutional Arrangements for Post-Disaster Recovery: Case Studies.*

Risk Assessment

Following a disaster, vulnerability and exposure to future hazards may significantly alter as a result of environmental and earth processes (e.g., changes to topography and coastlines) and socioeconomic impacts (e.g., loss of livelihoods and assets, reduced social safety net). Additionally, there may be an improved understanding of natural hazards (e.g., identification of new fault lines, changes in expected ground acceleration, new liquefaction zones, or updates to return periods for extreme weather events), especially if measures such as hazard monitoring systems and post-disaster damage assessments have been implemented. In these situations, it is particularly critical to ensure that existing hazard maps and quantitative risk models are updated and that comprehensive multihazard risk assessments are undertaken to inform recovery and reconstruction activities. These should take place as soon as possible so that there is adequate information on necessary land-use alterations and new siting of infrastructure, for instance. Risk assessments should include all relevant natural multihazard risks rather than only those which recently occurred. An example is provided in Box 2.

Box 2: Project Example—Revised Risk Assessment and Hazard Mapping Following the Great East Japan Earthquake

Prior to the Great East Japan Earthquake of 2011, Japan's Central Disaster Management Council had established a committee responsible for hazard modeling and disaster response planning. The committee undertook an assessment of trench-type events in the location of the 2011 earthquake. However, its models were prepared based on a limited selection of historic earthquake scenarios. Despite events on a much larger scale having been previously observed, these were excluded from the modeling due to data limitations and low likelihood.

The 2011 earthquake had a very large epicentral and tsunami source area and a moment magnitude of 9.0. Each of these features exceeded any earthquake that had been monitored in Japan's history. As such, the extent of the high seismic intensity area was approximately 10 times greater than expected, with the height of the tsunami at around double what was predicted. Damage far exceeded pre-disaster estimates, with the number of buildings destroyed and lives lost being six to seven times higher than anticipated. Therefore, the Government of Japan has since revised its earthquake and tsunami assessment methods based on the principle that countermeasures should be designed on scenarios that consider (i) the largest-possible earthquakes and tsunamis, considered from every possible angle; and (ii) the most comprehensive earthquake records available, in combination with analyses of the literature, topographic and geologic studies, and other scientific findings. Following the earthquake, the Japanese government created a new legislative framework that mandates the use of tsunami inundation maps to regulate land-use planning, in addition to municipal hazard maps that are based on updated hazard models.

Source: Adapted from World Bank. 2012. Risk Assessment and Hazard Mapping. *Knowledge Note 5-1, Cluster 5: Hazard and Risk Information and Decision Making.*

A variety of tools and methodologies for disaster risk assessments are available with varying applications, contexts, and scales at the national, subnational, and project levels. Each should be selected based on scope and objectives; relevant data and technology; available resources (i.e., time, expertise, and funding); and stakeholder and end-user priorities and concerns. Methods vary, from semi-qualitative and participatory assessments to highly quantitative data-driven assessments, based on statistics and modeling. A multihazard risk assessment should account for systemic risks across multiple infrastructure sectors and societal systems, factoring changes in exposure and vulnerability due to environmental, demographic, and social trends, and improved construction based on lessons learned. ADB and other development partners can provide technical assistance to determine the appropriate scope and scale of a risk assessment and support for implementation, where appropriate.

Multihazard assessments can inform risk-zoning maps to help inform improved land use planning, building regulations, and identify zones that would require additional resource allocation as part of recovery and reconstruction. Such maps should be readily available in electronic formats, easy to understand for all stakeholders, and should also clearly identify the limitations and uncertainties of the information they contain.

In the event of insufficient time to complete a full-scale quantitative multihazard risk assessment ahead of initiating reconstruction, at the least, a rapid screening of climate and natural hazard risks should be undertaken. Project financing and implementation arrangements, including terms of reference, should provide for a full disaster risk assessment during the implementation phase to inform project activities including infrastructure planning and design. Further guidance is available in ADB's *Disaster Risk Assessment for Project Preparation: A Practical Guide* (2017).

Key data sources to inform multihazard risk assessment following a disaster include remote sensing (satellite) imagery; national and regional risk monitors (e.g., strong motion data for earthquakes, rain gauges for floods, and displacement monitoring sensors for landslides); and data that have been captured as part of a post-disaster needs assessment. It is key that such data is electronically stored and statistically analyzed to provide insights on the impact of the event. Technology for capturing and processing real-time data on disaster impacts and recovery has proliferated in recent years, supported by on-ground assessments to confirm accuracy. Such applications can be useful to inform short-term response, as well as medium- and long-term socioeconomic recovery (Box 3). In many cases, ADB and other development agencies may be able to provide technical assistance, as well as leverage partnerships with international organizations to provide rapid access to situational data such as Earth Observation data from the European Space Agency.

Box 3: Remote Sensing Data for Assessment of Real-Time Disaster Impact on Socioeconomic Losses

When disaster strikes, government agencies require reliable and readily available information about impacts from the event so that they can take informed decisions about where to respond, how, and who to target in their operations. Such information is also critical to start mobilizing domestic and external resources that are needed for the immediate response and, later, recovery. Speed is of the essence, as delayed response to tropical cyclones, floods, earthquakes, droughts, epidemics, and other events can result in significant costs to households, governments, and the economy at large. Early and proactive disaster response, in turn, can help households protect their assets and avoid loss of income and its knock-on effects. It thus has the potential to bring down the price tag for response, recovery, and rehabilitation.[a]

Remote sensing and other Big Data provide a promising emerging source of relevant information on the socioeconomic impacts of disasters at relatively low cost and in real time through nowcasting, or even in advance of a disaster through impact-based forecasting to enable a timely response. It is important to note that these sources still face limitations and must be combined with other accurate data sources (such as data on land-use and digital elevation models) to inform findings. Even with advanced artificial intelligence processing techniques, remote sensing data also always requires expert validation, which can be challenging to provide in the post-disaster context.

The Asian Development Bank knowledge and support technical assistance **Nowcasting and Disasters: Impact-Based Forecasting and Socioeconomic Monitoring** (54113-001),[b] funded by the Japan Fund for Poverty Reduction, explores several applications of remote sensing data and other big data in socioeconomic impact assessment. Learning from retrospective country-disaster case studies, the methods can become a component in a "nowcasting tool" to estimate the immediate losses from disasters in different sectors. The impact and needs assessment can be refined as images and survey information become accessible over time.

In one study,[b] the impact of tropical cyclones on agriculture in Fiji is estimated by measuring the vegetation cover derived from satellite images, before and after the event, and linked with available household surveys and agricultural census data to assess economic impact. An automated tool kit for extraction and processing of satellite imagery, and construction of vegetation indices is being discussed with geographic information system experts in Fiji. Looking forward, with more granular and detailed datasets, the analysis paves a possible approach for estimating the predicted impact of a tropical cyclone on the agriculture sector of a cyclone-prone region, based only on the cyclone's known trajectory, and even before post-event satellite imagery becomes available.

Another case study in 2012 identifies the main fishing grounds in the Philippines' exclusive economic zone and examines the impact of tropical cyclone speed on fishing vessel position using satellite images and tropical cyclones data.[c] Indeed, analysis suggests that tropical cyclones have a negative impact on fishing activity with fewer active boats during and after the storm, and, consequently, a reduction in fishing commercial production. Repeated monitoring of such trends of disaster impacts in areas where people and assets are highly exposed to disasters can feed into hazard preparedness frameworks and inform immediate and long-term strategies to prevent loss of livelihoods.

continued on next page

Box 3 *continued*

Another useful avenue is human mobility data—mobile phone and global positioning system data—that can provide rapid information to understand the impact of a disaster. After a 6.5 magnitude earthquake struck Maluku Island, Indonesia in September 2019, mobility data showed a significant drop in human activity within a 10-kilometer radius from the epicenter on the day of the earthquake and a low activity profile in the following days.[d] Mobility data combined with information on infrastructure such as hospitals, commercial centers, schools, airports, train stations, etc. gives a detailed picture of areas of significant activity, disruption, and displacement, which can be used to inform recovery and preparedness for future disasters.[e]

[a]   See for example R. Hill, E. Skoufias, and B. Maher. 2019. The Chronology of a Disaster. A Review of the Value of Acting Early on Household Welfare; C. Cabot Venton. 2020. Economics of Early Response and Resilience to COVID-19: *Ethiopia*. SPACE; and C. Cabot Venton et al. 2012. The Economics of Early Response and Disaster Resilience: Lessons from Kenya and Ethiopia.
[b]   ADB. Regional: Nowcasting and Disasters: Impact-Based Forecasting and Socioeconomic Monitoring.
[c]   I. Noy et al. 2023. Nowcasting from Space: Tropical Cyclones' Impacts on Fiji's Agriculture. *Natural Hazards*. 4 July; and ADB. 2023. Appraising New Damage Assessment Techniques in Disaster-Prone Fiji.
[d]   ADB. 2023. The Impact of Tropical Cyclones on Fishing Activities in the Philippines.
[e]   M. Pundit and P. Villanueva. 2022. Tracking People's Movement after Disasters Can Save Lives. *Asian Development Blog*. 11 July.

Source: Asian Development Bank.

Early Warning Systems

Early warning systems (EWS) are central to manage residual risks associated with the exposure and vulnerability of communities, livelihoods, and key sectors to natural hazards, and contribute to climate change adaptation. As per the World Meteorological Organization, multihazard EWS are defined as an integrated system of four key elements that provide an end-to-end, people-centered services: (i) risk knowledge, (ii) monitoring and warning services, (iii) dissemination and communication, and (iv) response capability. These integrated processes enable individuals, communities, governments, businesses, and others to take timely action to anticipate and reduce disaster impacts.[8] The primary objective of EWS is to empower individuals and communities to respond and make informed decisions. In many cases, the cost of developing EWS is extremely low compared to the amount of loss that can be prevented with a functional EWS in operation.

There is an opportunity following a disaster to evaluate EWS adequacy and performance, as well as determine areas for improvement, such as (i) extending the lead time of warnings, (ii) improving the accuracy of warnings, (iii) greater demand for probabilistic forecasts, (iv) improving communication and the dissemination of warnings, (v) using new technologies to alert the public, (vi) targeting warning services to specific users (including the "last mile"), and (vii) transmitting clear warning and response messages for appropriate response.[9] It is essential to understand the performance of EWS in light of community requirements, and to explore opportunities for community-based early warning systems.

---

[8]   United Nations. 2017. Report of the Open-Ended Intergovernmental Expert Working Group on Indicators and Terminology Relating to Disaster Risk Reduction.
[9]   World Meteorological Organization. 2010. Guidelines on Early Warning Systems and Application of Nowcasting and Warning Operations. *PWS-21, WMO/TD*. No. 1559.

Investments in EWS should be considered strategically as they require the engagement of several stakeholders, and should take into account network integration across sectors, legal and policy frameworks, coordinating and/or cooperating partnerships across boundaries, sustained operations and maintenance (O&M) costs, and capacity-building requirements. Box 4 highlights details of EWS projects in Cambodia and India.

Box 4: Project Examples of Early Warning Systems

Kolkata's flood forecasting and early warning system (EWS), supported by the Asian Development Bank (ADB) under the **India: Kolkata Environment Improvement Investment Program**[a] (42266-025), responds to the long-term impacts of chronic seasonal flooding and is India's first comprehensive city-level early warning system. The EWS can provide forecasts and real-time updates on rainfall and inundation levels, among other climate and environmental data, via a network of sensors installed throughout the city. It uses web and mobile applications messaging system to provide warnings and real-time information to city officials and citizens.[a]

In August 2011, relentless rain caused the Mekong River and Tonlé Sap Lake to swell, and typhoons Nesat and Nalgae created further heavy monsoon rains, prompting the worst period of flooding in decades and affecting 18 of Cambodia's 24 provinces. ADB financed the **Cambodia: Flood Damage Emergency Reconstruction Project** (46009-001)[b] to support rehabilitation and reconstruction. Following further serious flash floods in 2013, ADB provided additional financing to support EWS reconstruction and strengthening. This included the installation of 10 hydromet and eight automatic weather stations to provide real-time measurement of river water levels and rainfall at strategically important locations, capacity building to manage the stations, support for data collection, and installation of EWS for communities and line agencies.

[a] ADB. India: Kolkata Environmental Improvement Investment Program—Tranche 2.
[b] ADB. Cambodia: Flood Damage Emergency Reconstruction Project.

Source: Asian Development Bank.

Land-Use Planning

Reducing the exposure of people and the built environment to hazards is a critical first step in disaster risk reduction. Post-disaster, it is important to consider carefully whether to reinstate communities and infrastructure in hazard-prone areas, particularly along coastlines and floodplains.

Accurate and updated multihazard maps, revised land-use plans with effective zoning, legislation and permit procedures, and strategies such as buy-back and land-swap schemes and relocation incentives are essential tools to manage construction and reconstruction in high-risk areas and reduce risks. Land acquisition and community resettlement should be considered as a last resort with careful reflection of social issues and community needs. Resettlement may be ineffective or harmful without attention to the culture and livelihoods of people, the environment, and multihazard risks in proposed resettlement locations. Additionally, resettlements should consider the conditions of nonengineered (informal) settlements and incorporate provisions to reduce the heightened risk to these communities, which likely exists as a result of poor planning and construction quality.

Ensuring that communities are well informed and are involved in land-use planning revisions is critical, not only to gain information of the local risks but also to secure buy-in and prevent the perpetuation of socioeconomic inequity. Well-intended land-use planning measures may fail if local people lack awareness and are excluded from the decision-making process. Furthermore, DMCs and local authorities often lack the necessary resources and capacity to enforce new (and existing) land use plans and guidelines. On the other hand, participatory land-use planning approaches that provide insights into current incentives and disincentives for communities and local governments to invest in land use regulations can identify and address the reasons behind the inertia of designing or implementing land use plans and lead to positive outcomes. Furthermore, information sharing on disaster risks and exploring the significance of land use plans for the resilience of communities and livelihoods can facilitate the engagement of stakeholders and decision-makers in disaster risk management efforts.

For example, following the 2004 Indian Ocean tsunami, 2009 Samoa tsunami, and 2018 Sulawesi earthquake and tsunami (Box 5), damage was partly driven by insufficient consideration of coastal risk in land-use planning, thus requiring the relocation of coastal communities further inland to prevent future impact.[10] Community consultation and engagement was central to this process.

Box 5: Project Example—Land-Use Planning
Following the 2018 Central Sulawesi Earthquake and Tsunami

In September 2018, a 7.5 magnitude earthquake struck Central Sulawesi, Indonesia, triggering 1.5-meter tsunami waves that caused widespread damage to Palu and Donggala. The event caused 2,081 fatalities; displaced 200,000 people; and severely damaged housing, infrastructure, and livelihoods. Government estimates of damage and loss reached 24.11 trillion rupiah ($1.70 billion equivalent). In response to the earthquake, the National Development Planning Agency requested support from development partners for a reconstruction master plan. The Asian Development Bank (ADB) provided technical assistance grants from various sources to support the undertaking of a post-disaster needs assessment, preparation of the reconstruction master plan, and development of a framework to monitor implementation.[a]

Recognizing that some liquefaction and tsunami-prone areas in Central Sulawesi were not suitable for reconstruction, the master plan identified relocation sites. Ground surveys, stakeholder consultation, and risk assessments were undertaken to inform a "Disaster Prone Zone" map, Peta Zona Rawan Bencana Palu dan Sekitarnya, which classified the level of vulnerability to natural hazards into four categories to guide recovery and reconstruction planning.

[a] Technical assistance grants were provided from various sources, including (i) the ADB-administered Urban Climate Change Resilience Trust Fund, financed by the governments of the United Kingdom and Switzerland and by The Rockefeller Foundation; (ii) Southeast Asia Urban Services Facility; and (iii) the Sustainable Infrastructure Assistance Program Phase II, financed by the Government of Australia.

Source: Asian Development Bank.

---

[10] S. Mannakkara and S. Wilkinson. 2013. "Build Back Better" Principles for Land-Use Planning. *Proceedings of the Institution of Civil Engineers Urban Design and Planning.* 166 (5). pp. 288–295.

Integrated Flood Risk Management

By 2050, around 80% of people in East and Southeast Asia will be impacted by sea-level rise and other climate-related hazards.[11] Reducing vulnerability and exposure to flooding and coastal hazards through integrated risk management is a critical aspect of almost every post-disaster recovery and reconstruction process.

The process of integrated flood risk management (IFRM) is a framework that promotes sustainable, long-term flood resilience by combining a range of solutions including social, economic, financial, environmental, and institutional measures; as well as engineering, disaster preparedness, insurance, and emergency response. As part of a recovery process, IFRM should aim to establish a strategy to reduce the economic, societal, and environmental cost of river basin and coastal zone flooding and erosion to acceptable levels. The key elements of IFRM are as follows:

(i)   Manage the entire water cycle, considering all flooding sources, and integrate the management of land and water (since these can contribute to the risk of flooding).
(ii) Adopt a multihazard approach that integrates IFRM with other risk reduction measures.
(iii) Adopt the best mix of measures, structural as well as nonstructural, to not only reduce the risk of flooding but also to mitigate the consequences in the event of a flood.
(iv) Ensure a participatory approach to encourage ownership of the strategy to reduce community exposure and vulnerability.

Following a disaster, there is frequently a need to revise flood risk management plans, incorporating lessons learned from previous disasters. Documentation of the extent of the flooded area and the level of flooding should be undertaken, as well as an update of flood hazard maps to prepare against future flood events and inform land-use planning, evacuation routes, and emergency shelters. This should be informed by a flood risk assessment. The plan and its proposed measures (including revisions to land use planning and policy) should account for all causes of failure in a flood risk management system, such as weak spots in structural protection and/or exceedance of design conditions.

Evaluation of a comprehensive portfolio of successive and systematic IFRM measures should be guided by the following principles: (i) reducing flood risks, (ii) protecting against floods to an agreed level of protection, (iii) regulating and adapting land use, (iv) raising awareness and preparedness, and (v) managing residual risk. Each of the measures usually has a corresponding policy and management area. Since IFRM cannot be implemented in isolation, it is crucial to integrate with other policy domains, given that post-disaster recovery efforts can provide room to review other aspects of disaster risk governance. Box 6 summarizes a wide portfolio of structural and governance measures for IFRM adopted for post-disaster recovery following the 2014 Pakistan floods.

---

[11]   R. Muggah. 2019. The World's Coastal Cities Are Going Under. Here's How Some Are Fighting Back. *World Economic Forum*. 16 January.

Box 6: Project Example—Integrated Flood Risk Management Following the 2014 Pakistan Floods

The Asian Development Bank (ADB) **Pakistan Flood Emergency Reconstruction and Resilience Project (49038-001)**[a] contributed to the economic and social recovery of flood-affected areas in Punjab Province and other affected districts following severe floods in 2014. The project outputs focused on the rehabilitation and reconstruction of damaged priority roads, bridges, irrigation, and flood protection infrastructure:

- The first output of the project reconstructed flood damaged roads and bridges in the Punjab Province and the districts of Haveli, Kotli, and Poonch to higher multihazard resilience standards.
- The second output focused on the reconstruction and upgrading of damaged irrigation, drainage, and flood protection schemes, including upgrading of priority flood protection schemes in the flood affected districts of Punjab to multihazard resilience standards (pictured below). Build back better was central to the subproject selection criteria with all infrastructure built to higher standards of disaster resilience.
- The third output encompassed the strengthening of disaster risk management through (i) human and institutional capacity development and strengthening the interface with the districts (downward) and other mandated institutions (horizontal and upward), which have a key role in flood risk management; and (ii) multihazard risk assessment data and system development.

The ADB project provided much-needed livelihoods opportunities, predominantly for women, in the growth and planting of millions of trees in steeply sloping areas and locations affected by landslides as a bioengineering measure to reduce the likelihood of future slope instability.

Following subsequent devastating floods in Pakistan from June to October 2022, ADB carried forward lessons learned from the 2014 flood recovery into its support for post-disaster recovery and reconstruction,[b] including in areas relating to donor coordination and engagement, pooling of resources, leveraging partnerships, comprehensive studies on disaster risk to inform planning and design, and integration with existing sector strategies.

[a] ADB. 2019. Pakistani Women Plant Millions of Trees to Rebuild Climate Resilient Roads. Video. 22 August.
[b] ADB. Pakistan: 2022 Flood Emergency Response; and ADB. Pakistan: Emergency Flood Assistance Project.

Source: Asian Development Bank.

Resilient Building and Infrastructure Standards

Resilient building and infrastructure regulations that account for disaster and climate risk are critical to inform resilient post-disaster reconstruction. A major disaster can serve as a catalyst to reform codes and standards (collectively referred to as standards). The first step in this process is often to prepare or update a comprehensive national multihazard risk assessment, including updated hazard maps (section III-B). Participation and input from community stakeholders should be sought to ensure that revised standards are appropriate to local requirements and cultural context.

In the last 2 decades, there has been a global shift from prescriptive- to performance-based standards in relation to the design of infrastructure for natural hazard resilience. Performance-based standards require that a structure meets specific performance criteria (e.g., human life safety and damage control) when specified design events occur. They recognize that different types of buildings and infrastructure have different performance objectives that are met when disaster occurs. For example, a design approach that pursues continued occupancy of a dwelling during a major cyclone or earthquake will be different from an approach that only enables safe evacuation for the same event, or only specifies continued occupancy during a lower category cyclone. Apart from strengthening resilience, performance-based standards have a range of other benefits in that they allow for significant cost savings; flexibility to use new products and introduce innovative design techniques; and potentially less effort for maintenance of standards over time (e.g., updates may not be required if hazard reference data were to change, though may be still required as new data comes available on infrastructure performance).

The importance of reviewing and updating standards to improve the structural resilience of buildings and infrastructure following a disaster is widely understood; however, it can be challenging due to a variety of issues. There may be strong reluctance on the part of the public and private sectors to absorb the additional costs to rebuild to higher standards. In DMCs, enforcement of codes and standards to an acceptable level of resilience remains a major barrier. Successful examples of rolling out improved standards often involve phased approaches; long-term funding to cover the additional costs for structural improvements; capacity development; strengthening of enforcement roles and resourcing; as well as incentives to promote adoption (e.g., tax incentives and ability to charge higher rents or obtain better interest rates).

The adoption of enhanced standards also needs to be supported by a strong legal framework and capacity building for national practitioners and communities. For example, in Sri Lanka at the time of the Indian Ocean tsunami, enforcement of building codes was restricted to urban and suburban areas with low implementation in rural and coastal areas that were most affected by the disaster.[12] There are also often challenges in applying formal building codes to vernacular construction types that are more prevalent in rural areas. This issue can be addressed with a range of measures including developing guidelines for adapting building codes and engaging international best practice professionals to deliver capacity building on resilient construction to the engineering and construction industry, the informal construction sector, and community members.

---

[12]   S. Mannakkara and S. Wilkinson. 2013. "Build Back Better" Principles for Post-Disaster Structural Improvements. *Structural Survey*. 31 (4). pp. 314–327.

Lessons learned from past disasters in Asia and the Pacific demonstrate a discord between enhancing resilience standards and rapid post-disaster rebuilding. The 2007 Tsunami Evaluation Commission Synthesis Report[13] provides examples where time pressures have led to nonadherence to design and construction policies for buildings and infrastructure, resulting in increased community vulnerability. Consultations and capacity development on implementation and enforcement of stronger standards are important to engage local authorities; practitioners (e.g., engineers, architects, and builders); and communities alike. Quality assurance in design and construction is essential, particularly where updated standards require enhanced techniques or stronger materials.

Capacity Development on Resilient Buildings and Infrastructure

Community participation in planning, design, construction, and long-term O&M can help to ensure that repaired and reconstructed infrastructure and buildings will be resilient, meet local requirements, be operated and maintained in a risk-informed manner, and be more rapidly repaired when future disasters occur. Where livelihoods have been lost or disrupted, the provision of skills training on resilient-building practices can contribute to restoring income source, reduce out-migration, and offer new livelihood opportunities.

Local involvement and capacity-building needs are particularly significant with respect to housing. The majority of houses rebuilt in ADB DMCs are nonengineered buildings constructed by the homeowners themselves, which forms the basis for assisted self-recovery approaches. Homeowners can be supported through skills training; deployment of user-friendly guides that incorporate resilience measures; and other technical assistance (e.g., design support, construction monitoring and supervision) in safe and resilient construction techniques. Due to the technical nature of construction skills, it is essential that training is practical, goes beyond classroom settings, and includes hands-on participation. Research suggests that it is most effective to target individuals with prior experience in the crafts and trades.[14] The mobilization of engineers, architects, and professional builders as part of relief efforts is critical to enable homeowners in recovery efforts. In a post-disaster context, train-the-trainer approaches can be particularly effective to roll out rapid training for homeowners on affordable and resilient-building techniques. Self-recovery may be complemented by conditional financial support to encourage investment in safer but potentially pricier building materials.[15]

Capacity development should take a broad view, including understanding climate and disaster risk, classifying suitable infrastructure and building types, siting, design and construction techniques, O&M, and contingency management. A multihazard approach should include the full spectrum of disaster risks, including long seismic intervals that may not have been previously experienced, as well as future changes in frequency and intensity of extreme weather events due to climate change.

---

[13]   J. Cosgrave. 2007. *Synthesis Report Expanded Summary: Joint Evaluation of the International Response to the Indian Ocean Tsunami*. Tsunami Evaluation Coalition.

[14]   B. Hidayat and Z. Afif. 2017. Knowledge Transfer to Builders in Post-Disaster Housing Reconstruction in West-Sumatra of Indonesia. *AIP Conference Proceedings*. 1903. pp. 110004-1–110004-7.

[15]   Centre for Development and Emergency Practice. 2017. Building Safety in Post-Disaster Shelter Self-Recovery: A Review of Current Knowledge. Oxford Brookes University.

Those who have been affected by disasters should be included in the decision-making process and the design of capacity building initiatives. While not all people will be amenable to participating in every decision, it is necessary that local stakeholders, at least, are strongly represented. Gender inclusiveness should be ensured to enhance social resilience. An example in Pakistan is provided in Box 7.

Box 7: Project Example—Capacity Development on Resilient Buildings and Infrastructure

Following the 2005 Pakistan earthquake that left nearly 4 million people homeless, the Asian Development Bank delivered the **Pakistan: Earthquake-Displaced People Livelihood Restoration Program**[a] (40563-013). The program included the training of 783,314 people in seismic-compliant building design and construction techniques, which was overseen by the Earthquake Reconstruction and Rehabilitation Authority and partner nongovernment organizations. Stakeholder participation was considered a major strength of the program. Overall, 463,243 "safe houses" were constructed by adopting a user-build approach wherein untrained builders were taught to construct "well and safely."[b]

[a]　ADB. Pakistan: Earthquake-Displaced People Livelihood Restoration Program.
[b]　I. Davis and D. Alexander. 2016. *Recovery from Disaster*. Routledge.

Source: Asian Development Bank.

Strengthening Local Community Social Systems

Enhancing climate and disaster resilience by BBB is as much a social process as it is an engineering one. As outlined in section II, local engagement is critical to strengthen social capital by increasing risk understanding, identifying resilient development options, selecting and implementing recovery measures, and maintaining and adjusting these over time.[16] When recovery processes are led solely by external actors, there is a risk that social capital is undermined, and that social differentiation and inequity are exacerbated.

Disaster recovery provides an opportunity to work closely with community-based organizations and local committees, not only to help design a more resilient recovery process that meets local needs, but also to strengthen community roles and capacity to address and respond to future disasters. Community-based organizations and committees may include community development leadership bodies, livelihood-based societies (e.g., farmers or fishers), women's development societies and self-help groups, and water-user committees. In some cases, DRM committees may be present, although often these are—or should be—embedded within a group or organization that has a regular function. Working with subnational stakeholders and local community groups is necessary to draw lessons from experience and establish or strengthen preparedness and contingency plans that are suited to the local risk landscape. A sample case study of a community-driven development approach is in the Philippines, the Delivering Recovery through an Existing Community-Driven Development Program in the Philippines, is discussed in the next subsection.

---

[16]　E. Wilkinson and J. Twigg. 2018. *"Building Back Better:" A Resilient Caribbean after the 2017 Hurricanes*. Overseas Development Institute.

Embedding DRM in key local institutions, such as schools, is critical to building long-term resilience at the local level. For example, a school can include a plan of action for evacuation and establish safe zones (e.g., for vertical evacuation) or implement an earthquake preparedness training program. Embedding DRM within the school curriculum, furthermore, will ensure that children and teachers alike will better understand the risks and be able to act accordingly in the school, home, and wider community. Schools can play a central role within the community, including as evacuation centers.

Shock-Responsive Social Protection

Social protection is defined as a set of policies and programs designed to reduce poverty and vulnerability by promoting efficient labor markets, lessening people's exposure to risks, and strengthening their capacity to protect themselves against hazards and loss of income.[17] Social protection encompasses three major categories: (i) social assistance, (ii) social insurance, and (iii) labor market programs. Robust social protection systems leverage all three instruments to reduce vulnerabilities across the lifecycle. Given the increasing intensity and frequency of covariate shocks (large shocks that affect entire communities), the provision of shock-responsive and adaptive social protection has also become essential to build the resilience of vulnerable communities. Shock-responsive social protection is the use of social protection systems and programs to anticipate, mobilize, and rapidly expand in the instance of a shock or crisis to deliver vital income support to households. Adaptive social protection helps build the longer-term resilience of poor and vulnerable households by investing in their capacity to prepare for, cope with, and adapt to shocks, protecting their well-being and ensuring that they do not fall into or become trapped in poverty.[18] Adaptive and shock-responsive social protection tools integrate social protection with disaster risk management and climate adaptation to reduce both current and future risks and vulnerabilities.

A social protection system that is shock-responsive includes programs and systems that can be expanded in times of need as well as tapered off once recovery is underway. Vertical expansion refers to increasing benefits to existing social assistance beneficiaries, while horizontal expansion refers to adding new beneficiaries to the roster. The provision of timely support to vulnerable households can significantly reduce their risk of adopting negative coping strategies such as reducing food intake or selling off assets, which can have severe long-term impacts. To ensure that social protection responses can be quickly and effectively deployed, it is important to have policies (including financing instruments for scaling up), programs (such as cash transfers), and up-to-date systems in place. These systems, including social registries, national identification systems, early warning systems, and payment systems must also be linked together to capture the dynamic nature of poverty and vulnerability and allow for more accurate targeting and expansion of relevant programs.

The design of shock-responsive social protection should be informed by the nature of disasters and the way by which people have been affected. While cash support is generally preferred and can be used by households to meet individual needs, if supply chains are severely disrupted, food or other in-kind transfers may assist people in meeting their most basic needs. During the recovery and rehabilitation phase, cash may be the most appropriate method.

---

[17]   ADB. 2001. Social Protection Strategy.
[18]   ADB. 2022. Strategy 2030 Social Protection Directional Guide 2022–2030: Towards Inclusive and Resilient Social Protection.

The design of shock-responsive social protection measures should calculate the time it will take for benefits to be delivered, the level of benefits, and the duration. The digitization of social protection programs and processes can strengthen shock responsiveness.

A shock-responsive system will ideally leverage existing social assistance benefits and payment systems. For example, the Mongolia Shock-Responsive Social Protection Projects (Box 8), supported by ADB in response to the coronavirus disease (COVID-190 pandemic, built on a pre-existing universal child benefit by topping up the regular monthly payments into bank accounts set up in the name of each child, effectively reaching approximately 80% of the population with shock-responsive support in little time.

Box 8: Project Example—Shock-Responsive Social Protection

The 2020 **Mongolia: Shock-Responsive Social Protection Project**[a] (54214-001) of the Asian Development Bank (ADB) provided a $73 million loan to improve social welfare support for poor and vulnerable groups, especially women and children, and to mitigate the socioeconomic impacts of the coronavirus disease (COVID-19) pandemic in the country. By leveraging and expanding the existing national child money program, which provides universal cash grants to all children aged 0–17, the project was able to reach around two-thirds of all households with benefit top-ups. The project also included top-ups to a food stamp program targeted to the 5% poorest households. As the design built on existing programs and systems, all loan proceeds (aside from minor project management costs) were channeled directly to the transfers. Six months later, the government requested ADB to prepare a follow-on project that provided an opportunity to draw on lessons to strengthen shock-responsiveness for future disasters, including allowing horizontal expansion to poor and vulnerable households by updating the poverty targeting system and the Integrated Household Database, and supporting digitization of the social protection system.

The Second Shock-Responsive Social Protection Project (54214-002),[b] is also supporting the Government of Mongolia to pilot an innovative, holistic and proven approach to social protection for economic inclusion, also referred to as the Graduation Approach. The intervention provides social welfare benefits to poor households in addition to productive asset transfers and technical training, as well as coaching and psychosocial support to assist them in diversifying their livelihoods and sources of income, so they are better able to better withstand future shocks. Global evidence, including from an ADB-financed pilot in the Philippines highlighted that the graduation approach increased household resilience during the COVID-19 pandemic across a range of dimensions including financial security, food security, and mental health.[c] Strong positive results from similar programs implemented around the world suggests graduation programs can be considered as part of efforts to promote sustainable livelihoods and climate-resilience, including during shocks and disasters.

[a] ADB. Mongolia: Shock-Responsive Social Protection Project.
[b] ADB. Mongolia: Second Shock-Responsive Social Protection Project.
[c] K. Schelzig and A. Jilani. 2021. Assessing the Impact of the Graduation Approach in the Philippines. *ADB Briefs* No. 169.

Source: Asian Development Bank.

ADB Philippines: KALAHI-CIDSS National Community-Driven Development Project (46420-002), Social Protection Support Project (Additional Financing) (43407-014), and Countercyclical Support Loan (43300-013). Beneficiaries of social assistance programs in Barangay Salvacion, Pilar, Surigao Del Norte.

Resilient Livelihood Recovery

The restoration and improvement of livelihoods following disasters is critical to strengthen resilience. Furthermore, rapid livelihood restoration will enable those affected to fund their own recovery to the extent possible, thus resulting in a multiplier effect on the local economy. When livelihoods are not sufficiently supported, recovery from disaster can be extremely challenging. Debt burdens and an inability to recover lost productive assets can have the longest impacts on recovery aspirations.

In general, the course of action toward rebuilding resilient livelihoods should ensure that household income sources are increased and that shortfalls are supplemented to mitigate loss in periods of shock or stress. Key opportunities include the following:

(i) **Provide access to credit and financial services to strengthen the resilience of affected households**. Microcredit schemes are one example, as is working with the private sector and mobile money operators for flexible pro-poor products.

(ii) **Provide income opportunities in the short term when livelihood restoration cannot quickly be restored**. Often in the aftermath of a disaster, the immediate and widespread need for reconstruction can be leveraged to activate local labor markets and lessen economic impacts. In addition to labor-intensive reconstruction activities, there can be a need to create other cash-for-work opportunities for women and men. Short-term income prospects and livelihood opportunities should be linked to build long-term resilience.

(iii) **For relevant projects, consider providing access to agricultural inputs.** These include seeds for high-value and high-yielding crop varieties to strengthen livelihood resilience, taking into account climate change and disaster risks such as increasing salinity and aridity.

(iv) **Prioritize the restoration of facilities and amenities that are the mainstay of livelihoods**. For example, in the case of the 2013 Uttarakhand flood and landslide disaster in India, restoration of tourism facilities was prioritized as local livelihoods were highly dependent on tourism.

(v) **Alleviate pressure on household income and improve household nutrition**. Village or rural cooperatives should be supported with the planting of fruit trees, vegetable gardens, and apiaries, all of which should be resilient to climate change and disasters.

(vi) **Support the diversification of livelihoods.** Offer new livelihood options that are suited to the local climate and hazards and can supplement insecure agriculture income due to climate or disaster impacts. This can, for instance, be in the form of microenterprise activities that can be undertaken at home and that helps to spread risks.

A project case study that outlines multiple concepts covered in this volume including resilient livelihood recovery, community-driven development approaches, and capacity building is outlined in Box 9.

Box 9: Case Study—Delivering Recovery through an Existing Community-Driven Development Program in the Philippines

Typhoon Haiyan, known locally as "Yolanda," hit central Philippines on 8 November 2013. The final damage report indicated a death toll of more than 7,000 and 28,000 injured. About 890,000 families, or 4.1 million people, were displaced. The government estimated the damage at $2.2 billion. The Asian Development Bank (ADB) estimated that 1.5 million people may have fallen into poverty immediately following the typhoon.

To support recovery and rehabilitation efforts, the Philippines' Department of Social Welfare and Development expanded the existing *Kapit-Bisig Laban sa Kahirapan* (Linking Arms Against Poverty): Comprehensive and Integrated Delivery of Social Services system, or KALAHI-CIDSS. KALAHI-CIDSS is a nationwide and community-driven development government program that began in 2003. Its objectives are to improve service delivery, local governance, and community empowerment. KALAHI-CIDSS covered approximately 90% of the Yolanda-affected areas and, with its well-established operating system, was able to channel the necessary funding and technical support for community programs and social services.

On 16 December 2013, ADB approved a $372.1 million emergency assistance loan for the **Philippines: KALAHI–CIDSS National Community-Driven Development Project**[a] (46420-002), or KC-NCDDP, to restore basic social services and rebuild communities through the expansion of the KALAHI–CIDSS in 512 municipalities affected by Typhoon Yolanda. The project loan became effective on 10 June 2014 (7 months following the typhoon) and ran until 30 June 2018. The project's expected impact was improved resilience of poor communities to natural hazards. The expected outcome was improved access to services and infrastructure for communities in affected provinces and their participation in more inclusive local disaster risk reduction and management planning, budgeting, and implementation.

April 2014, ADB also provided a $20 million grant from the Japan Fund for Poverty Reduction to aid post-Haiyan rehabilitation efforts and to provide emergency employment and livelihood assistance. In March 2016, ADB approved an additional grant of $5 million from the Typhoon Yolanda

continued on next page

Box 9 *continued*

KALAHI-CIDSS National Community-Driven Development Project in the Philippines | 43407-014: Social Protection Support Project (Additional Financing) in the Philippines | 43300-013: Countercyclical Support Loan in the Philippines. Beneficiaries of the 4Ps program plant vegetables in community gardens around Barangay Katipunan, Pilar, Surigao Del Norte.

Multi-Donor Trust Fund for various innovative livelihood and enterprise subprojects in 262 municipalities. The additional activities sought to address the challenges that were not considered in the original design. The outcome was transformational and enabled the affected communities to restore their livelihoods as well as community infrastructure.

Capitalizing on a well-established management system and delivery mechanism strengthened the relevance of the project; however some adjustments were required. The KC-NCDDP normally follows an 8–12-month cycle that includes project preparation, community planning, community-led subproject design, implementation, and evaluation. To address the post-disaster needs of communities, the KC-NCDDP project initially applied a shortened planning and implementation cycle to accelerate the fund transfer and delivery of services to typhoon-affected areas. This allowed greater flexibility in responding to the emergency through existing resources and systems, including a network of trained facilitators, community committees, and volunteers, thus accelerating community response during early recovery and rehabilitation.

Of the 15,541 subprojects, 10,010 (64%) adopted the Disaster Response Operations Modality to repair and rehabilitate structures damaged by the typhoon and to build resilient facilities. Subprojects included repair and construction of roads and footpaths, classrooms, and water and sanitation systems. A major achievement was the increase of awareness in poor communities of climate and disaster risks. Over 300,000 volunteers were trained (nearly 200,000 of whom were women) in situational analyses and needs identification, preparation of project proposals, financial management and procurement, and subproject implementation.

Community-driven development approaches may require intensive involvement of service providers, technical agencies, and the provision of capacity building for both communities and program staff. International experience indicates an optimal initial ratio of 50:50 for funds spent on subproject grants to funds for capacity support and monitoring of 50:50, transitioning to 75:25 in favor of subproject grants in subsequent years.

[a]   ADB. Philippines: KALAHI-CIDSS National Community-Driven Development Project.

Source: Asian Development Bank.

ADB Philippines: KALAHI-CIDSS National Community-Driven Development Project (46420-002), Social Protection Support Project (Additional Financing) (43407-014), and Countercyclical Support Loan (43300-013). An elementary student crossing a foot bridge in Barangay Katipunan, Pilar, Surigao del Norte. Funded by the ADB and the WB through the Kalahi-CIDDS program, the bridges in the village made walking to school safer for children.

ADB Vanuatu: Cyclone Pam Road Reconstruction Project (49319-001). The Cyclone Pam Road Reconstruction Project will help in the reconstruction of the transport sector infrastructure on Efate ring road damaged by the Cyclone Pam floods and storm surges during March 2015.

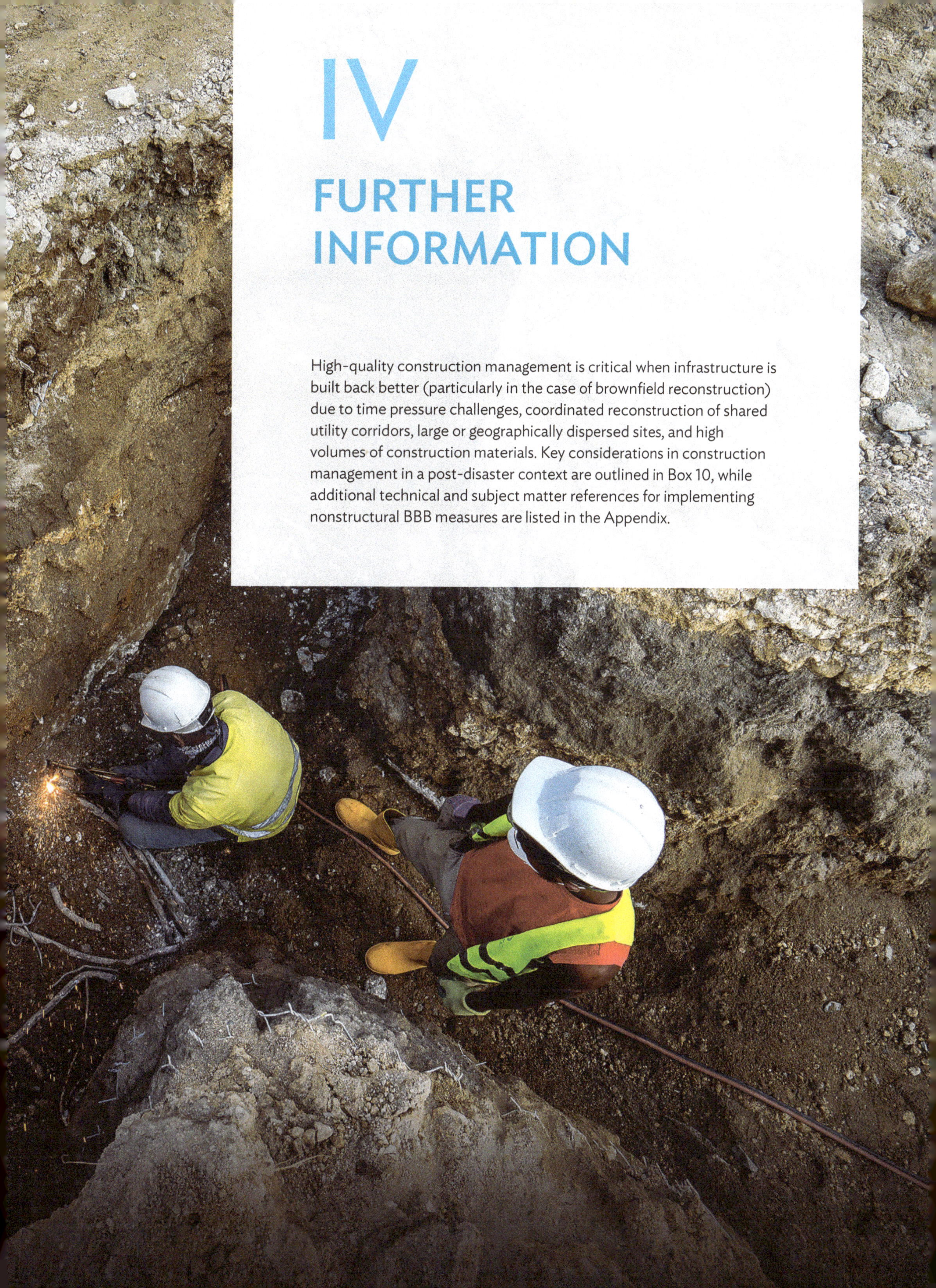

IV
FURTHER INFORMATION

High-quality construction management is critical when infrastructure is built back better (particularly in the case of brownfield reconstruction) due to time pressure challenges, coordinated reconstruction of shared utility corridors, large or geographically dispersed sites, and high volumes of construction materials. Key considerations in construction management in a post-disaster context are outlined in Box 10, while additional technical and subject matter references for implementing nonstructural BBB measures are listed in the Appendix.

Box 10: Construction Management in a Post-Disaster Context

High-quality construction management is critical when infrastructure is reinstated to higher levels of resilience (particularly in the case of brownfield reconstruction), yet can be highly challenging due to time pressure, coordinated reconstruction of shared utility corridors, large or geographically dispersed sites, and high volumes of construction materials. Following a disaster, it may be necessary to accelerate the reconstruction of critical infrastructure to reinstate access to communities and enable restoration of other key assets and services. Lessons from the Asian Development Bank emergency assistance loan project completion reports, however, demonstrate that accelerating capital works without adequate cross-sector coordination and quality control potentially will lead to low-quality works, economic loss in the long term, further disruption and downtime, and reduced safety.

Construction management during post-disaster recovery and reconstruction should account for the following considerations to ensure resilience objectives are achieved:

- **Materials**. Construction material requirements should be evaluated and coordinated by sector stakeholders. Priority should be given to locally sourced and sustainable materials (including building rubble where available) with environmental impacts minimized (e.g., overextraction of water for road subsurface preparation).
- **Coordination**. A "dig-once" policy should be introduced in coordination with relevant public work departments and private sector utility providers. Joint trench agreements should be established between parties with clear cost-sharing arrangements.
- **Scheduling**. Project timelines should be adequate for the review of designs, allowing more time for those structures that are complex and which require more stringent safety standards (particularly elevated structures). Construction timelines should be such as to ensure quality construction and workforce safety, as well as prevent potential natural hazards (e.g., monsoon season).
- **Supervision**. International quality control expertise should be considered for project design and resourcing, as well as inspection and testing of materials. Workforce capacity should be enhanced as required; and supervision, oversight, quality control, and verification of onsite construction and road safety should be assured.
- **Communities**. Road detours should be safe and reliable, temporary works and diversions carefully managed, and impacts on local communities minimized. Consideration should be given to community evacuation and access to emergency shelters in case of further event impacts during reconstruction.

Source: Asian Development Bank.

SUGGESTED READINGS

The following technical and subject matter resources are further references in implementing nonstructural BBB measures.

Asian Development Bank (ADB). 2018. Scaling Up Resilience—Building Measures through Community-Driven Development Projects: Guidance Note.

ADB. 2020. Assessing the Enabling Environment for Disaster Risk Financing: A Country Diagnostics Toolkit.

ADB. 2020. Financing Disaster Risk Reduction in Asia and the Pacific. A Guide for Policymakers.

ADB. 2021. Strengthening Integrated Flood Risk Management—Managing Uncertainty in Integrated Flood Risk Management using Dynamic Adaptive Pathways Planning.

ADB. 2022. A Practical Guide to Integrated Flood Risk Management.

ADB. 2022. Multilateral Development Bank Support for Disaster-Resilient Infrastructure Systems.

ADB. 2024. Disaster Risk Management Action Plan, 2024–2030: Redoubling Action Toward Disaster Resilience.

ALNAP. 2000. Participation by Crisis-Affected Populations in Humanitarian Action: A Handbook for Practitioners. Active Learning Network for Accountability and Performance in Humanitarian Action.

Associated Programme on Flood Management. 2016. The Role of Land-Use Planning in Flood Management. Integrated Flood Management Tools Series. No. 7.

Associated Programme on Flood Management. 2017. Selecting Measures and Designing Strategies for Integrated Flood Risk Management: A Guidance Document.

Green Climate Fund. 2023. Sectoral Guides. GCF Water Project Design Guidelines Annex II Water Security Sectoral Guide. Part 2: Applications of the Practical Guidelines for Designing Water-Climate Resilient Projects in IWRM, CR-WASH, and Drought and Flood Management.

S. Hallegatte, J. Rentschler, and B. Walsh. 2018. Building Back Better: Achieving Resilience through Stronger, Faster, and More Inclusive Post-Disaster Reconstruction. World Bank.

J. Matthews and E. Ocampo dela Cruz. 2022. Integrating Nature-Based Solutions for Climate Change Adaptation and Disaster Risk Management A Practitioner's Guide. Asian Development Bank.

R. Osti. 2018. Integrating Flood and Environmental Risk Management: Principles and Practices. *ADB East Asia Working Paper Series*. No. 15. Asian Development Bank.

M. Pundit and P. Villanueva. 2022. Tracking People's Movement after Disasters Can Save Lives. *Asian Development Blog*. 11 July.

United Nations Economic Commission for Europe and United Nations Office for Disaster Risk Reduction. 2018. *Words into Action Guidelines—Implementation Guide for Addressing Water-Related Disasters and Transboundary Cooperation: Integrating Disaster Risk Management with Water Management and Climate Change Adaptation.*

United Nations Office for Disaster Risk Reduction. 2017. Words into Action Guidelines: Build Back Better in Recovery, Rehabilitation and Reconstruction. Consultative Version.

United Nations Economic and Social Commission for Asia and the Pacific. 2009. What is Good Governance? Poverty Reduction Section, UNESCAP Bangkok.

ADB Tonga: Cyclone Gita Recovery Project (52129-001). Maintenance activities of energy infrastructure in Tonga. The Cyclone Gita Recovery Project reconstruct and climate- and disaster-proof the Nuku'alofa electricity network that was damaged by Tropical Cyclone Gita in February 2018.

www.ingramcontent.com/pod-product-compliance
Lightning Source LLC
LaVergne TN
LVHW071456180726
843512LV00018B/1398